Seen when walking our dog. Birds.

6" x 9" and 24 Pages of six birds per page (144 birds seen in the UK). Two spare pages at the end.

The dog's name is Tiddles and belongs to my best friends Jonathan and Julia Targett, whose walks, were the inspiration for this book. Also available are two more logbooks:-
"Seen on walking our dog. Insects", and
"Seen on walking our dog. Plants".

As this is a logbook, you may need a bird identification book for when you get home to be sure. Take a photo of the bird to make this easier.

Bird Name: Accentors	**Bird Name: Acciptors**
Identified ☐	Identified ☐
Where seen? On the:	Where seen? On the:
Ground ☐ Plant ☐ Bush ☐ Tree ☐	Ground ☐ Plant ☐ Bush ☐ Tree ☐
Flying ☐ Dead ☐	Flying ☐ Dead ☐
Male ☐ Female ☐ Adult ☐ Chick ☐	Male ☐ Female ☐ Adult ☐ Chick ☐
Details:- Date: ___/___/___ **Location: _______________________** **Bird Variant: _____________________**	**Details:- Date: ___/___/___** **Location: _______________________** **Bird Variant: _____________________**
Bird Name: Albatrosses	**Bird Name: American Sparrows**
Identified ☐	Identified ☐
Where seen? On the:	Where seen? On the:
Ground ☐ Plant ☐ Bush ☐ Tree ☐	Ground ☐ Plant ☐ Bush ☐ Tree ☐
Flying ☐ Dead ☐	Flying ☐ Dead ☐
Male ☐ Female ☐ Adult ☐ Chick ☐	Male ☐ Female ☐ Adult ☐ Chick ☐
Details:- Date: ___/___/___ **Location: _______________________** **Bird Variant: _____________________**	**Details:- Date: ___/___/___** **Location: _______________________** **Bird Variant: _____________________**
Bird Name: Auks	**Bird Name: Avocets**
Identified ☐	Identified ☐
Where seen? On the:	Where seen? On the:
Ground ☐ Plant ☐ Bush ☐ Tree ☐	Ground ☐ Plant ☐ Bush ☐ Tree ☐
Flying ☐ Dead ☐	Flying ☐ Dead ☐
Male ☐ Female ☐ Adult ☐ Chick ☐	Male ☐ Female ☐ Adult ☐ Chick ☐
Details:- Date: ___/___/___ **Location: _______________________** **Bird Variant: _____________________**	**Details:- Date: ___/___/___** **Location: _______________________** **Bird Variant: _____________________**

Bird Name: Babblers	**Bird Name: Barbets**
Identified ☐	Identified ☐
Where seen? On the:	Where seen? On the:
Ground ☐ Plant ☐ Bush ☐ Tree ☐	Ground ☐ Plant ☐ Bush ☐ Tree ☐
Flying ☐ Dead ☐	Flying ☐ Dead ☐
Male ☐ Female ☐ Adult ☐ Chick ☐	Male ☐ Female ☐ Adult ☐ Chick ☐
Details:- Date: ___/___/___ **Location: ______________________** **Bird Variant: ______________________**	**Details:- Date: ___/___/___** **Location: ______________________** **Bird Variant: ______________________**
Bird Name: Barn Owls	**Bird Name: Bearded Tits**
Identified ☐	Identified ☐
Where seen? On the:	Where seen? On the:
Ground ☐ Plant ☐ Bush ☐ Tree ☐	Ground ☐ Plant ☐ Bush ☐ Tree ☐
Flying ☐ Dead ☐	Flying ☐ Dead ☐
Male ☐ Female ☐ Adult ☐ Chick ☐	Male ☐ Female ☐ Adult ☐ Chick ☐
Details:- Date: ___/___/___ **Location: ______________________** **Bird Variant: ______________________**	**Details:- Date: ___/___/___** **Location: ______________________** **Bird Variant: ______________________**
Bird Name: Bee-Eaters	**Bird Name: Bishops**
Identified ☐	Identified ☐
Where seen? On the:	Where seen? On the:
Ground ☐ Plant ☐ Bush ☐ Tree ☐	Ground ☐ Plant ☐ Bush ☐ Tree ☐
Flying ☐ Dead ☐	Flying ☐ Dead ☐
Male ☐ Female ☐ Adult ☐ Chick ☐	Male ☐ Female ☐ Adult ☐ Chick ☐
Details:- Date: ___/___/___ **Location: ______________________** **Bird Variant: ______________________**	**Details:- Date: ___/___/___** **Location: ______________________** **Bird Variant: ______________________**

Bird Name: Bitterns	**Bird Name: Bulbuls**
Identified ☐	Identified ☐
Where seen? On the:	Where seen? On the:
Ground ☐ Plant ☐ Bush ☐ Tree ☐	Ground ☐ Plant ☐ Bush ☐ Tree ☐
Flying ☐ Dead ☐	Flying ☐ Dead ☐
Male ☐ Female ☐ Adult ☐ Chick ☐	Male ☐ Female ☐ Adult ☐ Chick ☐
Details:- Date: ___/___/___ **Location: _______________________** **Bird Variant: ___________________**	**Details:- Date: ___/___/___** **Location: _______________________** **Bird Variant: ___________________**
Bird Name: Buntings	**Bird Name: Bush Warbler**
Identified ☐	Identified ☐
Where seen? On the:	Where seen? On the:
Ground ☐ Plant ☐ Bush ☐ Tree ☐	Ground ☐ Plant ☐ Bush ☐ Tree ☐
Flying ☐ Dead ☐	Flying ☐ Dead ☐
Male ☐ Female ☐ Adult ☐ Chick ☐	Male ☐ Female ☐ Adult ☐ Chick ☐
Details:- Date: ___/___/___ **Location: _______________________** **Bird Variant: ___________________**	**Details:- Date: ___/___/___** **Location: _______________________** **Bird Variant: ___________________**
Bird Name: Bustards	**Bird Name: Buzzards**
Identified ☐	Identified ☐
Where seen? On the:	Where seen? On the:
Ground ☐ Plant ☐ Bush ☐ Tree ☐	Ground ☐ Plant ☐ Bush ☐ Tree ☐
Flying ☐ Dead ☐	Flying ☐ Dead ☐
Male ☐ Female ☐ Adult ☐ Chick ☐	Male ☐ Female ☐ Adult ☐ Chick ☐
Details:- Date: ___/___/___ **Location: _______________________** **Bird Variant: ___________________**	**Details:- Date: ___/___/___** **Location: _______________________** **Bird Variant: ___________________**

Bird Name: Cardinals	**Bird Name: Chats**
Identified ☐	Identified ☐
Where seen? On the:	Where seen? On the:
Ground ☐ Plant ☐ Bush ☐ Tree ☐	Ground ☐ Plant ☐ Bush ☐ Tree ☐
Flying ☐ Dead ☐	Flying ☐ Dead ☐
Male ☐ Female ☐ Adult ☐ Chick ☐	Male ☐ Female ☐ Adult ☐ Chick ☐
Details:- Date: ___/___/___ **Location: ____________________** **Bird Variant: __________________**	**Details:- Date: ___/___/___** **Location: ____________________** **Bird Variant: __________________**
Bird Name: Cisticolas	**Bird Name: Coots**
Identified ☐	Identified ☐
Where seen? On the:	Where seen? On the:
Ground ☐ Plant ☐ Bush ☐ Tree ☐	Ground ☐ Plant ☐ Bush ☐ Tree ☐
Flying ☐ Dead ☐	Flying ☐ Dead ☐
Male ☐ Female ☐ Adult ☐ Chick ☐	Male ☐ Female ☐ Adult ☐ Chick ☐
Details:- Date: ___/___/___ **Location: ____________________** **Bird Variant: __________________**	**Details:- Date: ___/___/___** **Location: ____________________** **Bird Variant: __________________**
Bird Name: Cormorants	**Bird Name: Coucals**
Identified ☐	Identified ☐
Where seen? On the:	Where seen? On the:
Ground ☐ Plant ☐ Bush ☐ Tree ☐	Ground ☐ Plant ☐ Bush ☐ Tree ☐
Flying ☐ Dead ☐	Flying ☐ Dead ☐
Male ☐ Female ☐ Adult ☐ Chick ☐	Male ☐ Female ☐ Adult ☐ Chick ☐
Details:- Date: ___/___/___ **Location: ____________________** **Bird Variant: __________________**	**Details:- Date: ___/___/___** **Location: ____________________** **Bird Variant: __________________**

Bird Name: Coursers	**Bird Name: Crakes**
Identified ☐	Identified ☐
Where seen? On the:	Where seen? On the:
Ground ☐ Plant ☐ Bush ☐ Tree ☐	Ground ☐ Plant ☐ Bush ☐ Tree ☐
Flying ☐ Dead ☐	Flying ☐ Dead ☐
Male ☐ Female ☐ Adult ☐ Chick ☐	Male ☐ Female ☐ Adult ☐ Chick ☐
Details:- Date: ___/___/___ **Location: _______________________** **Bird Variant: _______________________**	**Details:- Date: ___/___/___** **Location: _______________________** **Bird Variant: _______________________**
Bird Name: Cranes	**Bird Name: Creepers**
Identified ☐	Identified ☐
Where seen? On the:	Where seen? On the:
Ground ☐ Plant ☐ Bush ☐ Tree ☐	Ground ☐ Plant ☐ Bush ☐ Tree ☐
Flying ☐ Dead ☐	Flying ☐ Dead ☐
Male ☐ Female ☐ Adult ☐ Chick ☐	Male ☐ Female ☐ Adult ☐ Chick ☐
Details:- Date: ___/___/___ **Location: _______________________** **Bird Variant: _______________________**	**Details:- Date: ___/___/___** **Location: _______________________** **Bird Variant: _______________________**
Bird Name: Crows	**Bird Name: Cuckoos**
Identified ☐	Identified ☐
Where seen? On the:	Where seen? On the:
Ground ☐ Plant ☐ Bush ☐ Tree ☐	Ground ☐ Plant ☐ Bush ☐ Tree ☐
Flying ☐ Dead ☐	Flying ☐ Dead ☐
Male ☐ Female ☐ Adult ☐ Chick ☐	Male ☐ Female ☐ Adult ☐ Chick ☐
Details:- Date: ___/___/___ **Location: _______________________** **Bird Variant: _______________________**	**Details:- Date: ___/___/___** **Location: _______________________** **Bird Variant: _______________________**

Bird Name: Curlews	**Bird Name: Daters**
Identified ☐	Identified ☐
Where seen? On the:	Where seen? On the:
Ground ☐ Plant ☐ Bush ☐ Tree ☐	Ground ☐ Plant ☐ Bush ☐ Tree ☐
Flying ☐ Dead ☐	Flying ☐ Dead ☐
Male ☐ Female ☐ Adult ☐ Chick ☐	Male ☐ Female ☐ Adult ☐ Chick ☐
Details:- Date: ___/___/___ **Location:** _______________________ **Bird Variant:** _______________________	**Details:- Date:** ___/___/___ **Location:** _______________________ **Bird Variant:** _______________________
Bird Name: Dippers	**Bird Name: Divers**
Identified ☐	Identified ☐
Where seen? On the:	Where seen? On the:
Ground ☐ Plant ☐ Bush ☐ Tree ☐	Ground ☐ Plant ☐ Bush ☐ Tree ☐
Flying ☐ Dead ☐	Flying ☐ Dead ☐
Male ☐ Female ☐ Adult ☐ Chick ☐	Male ☐ Female ☐ Adult ☐ Chick ☐
Details:- Date: ___/___/___ **Location:** _______________________ **Bird Variant:** _______________________	**Details:- Date:** ___/___/___ **Location:** _______________________ **Bird Variant:** _______________________
Bird Name: Doves	**Bird Name: Drongoes**
Identified ☐	Identified ☐
Where seen? On the:	Where seen? On the:
Ground ☐ Plant ☐ Bush ☐ Tree ☐	Ground ☐ Plant ☐ Bush ☐ Tree ☐
Flying ☐ Dead ☐	Flying ☐ Dead ☐
Male ☐ Female ☐ Adult ☐ Chick ☐	Male ☐ Female ☐ Adult ☐ Chick ☐
Details:- Date: ___/___/___ **Location:** _______________________ **Bird Variant:** _______________________	**Details:- Date:** ___/___/___ **Location:** _______________________ **Bird Variant:** _______________________

Bird Name: Ducks	**Bird Name: Eagles**
Identified ☐	Identified ☐
Where seen? On the:	Where seen? On the:
Ground ☐ Plant ☐ Bush ☐ Tree ☐	Ground ☐ Plant ☐ Bush ☐ Tree ☐
Flying ☐ Dead ☐	Flying ☐ Dead ☐
Male ☐ Female ☐ Adult ☐ Chick ☐	Male ☐ Female ☐ Adult ☐ Chick ☐
Details:- Date: ___/___/___ **Location: ______________________** **Bird Variant: __________________**	**Details:- Date: ___/___/___** **Location: ______________________** **Bird Variant: __________________**
Bird Name: Egrets	**Bird Name: Estrilids**
Identified ☐	Identified ☐
Where seen? On the:	Where seen? On the:
Ground ☐ Plant ☐ Bush ☐ Tree ☐	Ground ☐ Plant ☐ Bush ☐ Tree ☐
Flying ☐ Dead ☐	Flying ☐ Dead ☐
Male ☐ Female ☐ Adult ☐ Chick ☐	Male ☐ Female ☐ Adult ☐ Chick ☐
Details:- Date: ___/___/___ **Location: ______________________** **Bird Variant: __________________**	**Details:- Date: ___/___/___** **Location: ______________________** **Bird Variant: __________________**
Bird Name: Falcons	**Bird Name: Finches**
Identified ☐	Identified ☐
Where seen? On the:	Where seen? On the:
Ground ☐ Plant ☐ Bush ☐ Tree ☐	Ground ☐ Plant ☐ Bush ☐ Tree ☐
Flying ☐ Dead ☐	Flying ☐ Dead ☐
Male ☐ Female ☐ Adult ☐ Chick ☐	Male ☐ Female ☐ Adult ☐ Chick ☐
Details:- Date: ___/___/___ **Location: ______________________** **Bird Variant: __________________**	**Details:- Date: ___/___/___** **Location: ______________________** **Bird Variant: __________________**

Bird Name: Finfoot	**Bird Name: Flamingos**
Identified ☐	Identified ☐
Where seen? On the:	Where seen? On the:
Ground ☐ Plant ☐ Bush ☐ Tree ☐	Ground ☐ Plant ☐ Bush ☐ Tree ☐
Flying ☐ Dead ☐	Flying ☐ Dead ☐
Male ☐ Female ☐ Adult ☐ Chick ☐	Male ☐ Female ☐ Adult ☐ Chick ☐
Details:- Date: ___/___/___ **Location: _____________________** **Bird Variant: ___________________**	**Details:- Date: ___/___/___** **Location: _____________________** **Bird Variant: ___________________**
Bird Name: Flycatchers	**Bird Name: Francolins**
Identified ☐	Identified ☐
Where seen? On the:	Where seen? On the:
Ground ☐ Plant ☐ Bush ☐ Tree ☐	Ground ☐ Plant ☐ Bush ☐ Tree ☐
Flying ☐ Dead ☐	Flying ☐ Dead ☐
Male ☐ Female ☐ Adult ☐ Chick ☐	Male ☐ Female ☐ Adult ☐ Chick ☐
Details:- Date: ___/___/___ **Location: _____________________** **Bird Variant: ___________________**	**Details:- Date: ___/___/___** **Location: _____________________** **Bird Variant: ___________________**
Bird Name: Frigatebirds	**Bird Name: Gallinules**
Identified ☐	Identified ☐
Where seen? On the:	Where seen? On the:
Ground ☐ Plant ☐ Bush ☐ Tree ☐	Ground ☐ Plant ☐ Bush ☐ Tree ☐
Flying ☐ Dead ☐	Flying ☐ Dead ☐
Male ☐ Female ☐ Adult ☐ Chick ☐	Male ☐ Female ☐ Adult ☐ Chick ☐
Details:- Date: ___/___/___ **Location: _____________________** **Bird Variant: ___________________**	**Details:- Date: ___/___/___** **Location: _____________________** **Bird Variant: ___________________**

Bird Name: Gannets	**Bird Name: Geese**
Identified ☐	Identified ☐
Where seen? On the:	Where seen? On the:
Ground ☐ Plant ☐ Bush ☐ Tree ☐	Ground ☐ Plant ☐ Bush ☐ Tree ☐
Flying ☐ Dead ☐	Flying ☐ Dead ☐
Male ☐ Female ☐ Adult ☐ Chick ☐	Male ☐ Female ☐ Adult ☐ Chick ☐
Details:- Date: ___/___/___ **Location: _______________________** **Bird Variant: _____________________**	**Details:- Date: ___/___/___** **Location: _______________________** **Bird Variant: _____________________**
Bird Name: Godwits	**Bird Name: Grasshopper Warblers**
Identified ☐	Identified ☐
Where seen? On the:	Where seen? On the:
Ground ☐ Plant ☐ Bush ☐ Tree ☐	Ground ☐ Plant ☐ Bush ☐ Tree ☐
Flying ☐ Dead ☐	Flying ☐ Dead ☐
Male ☐ Female ☐ Adult ☐ Chick ☐	Male ☐ Female ☐ Adult ☐ Chick ☐
Details:- Date: ___/___/___ **Location: _______________________** **Bird Variant: _____________________**	**Details:- Date: ___/___/___** **Location: _______________________** **Bird Variant: _____________________**
Bird Name: Grebes	**Bird Name: Greenbuls**
Identified ☐	Identified ☐
Where seen? On the:	Where seen? On the:
Ground ☐ Plant ☐ Bush ☐ Tree ☐	Ground ☐ Plant ☐ Bush ☐ Tree ☐
Flying ☐ Dead ☐	Flying ☐ Dead ☐
Male ☐ Female ☐ Adult ☐ Chick ☐	Male ☐ Female ☐ Adult ☐ Chick ☐
Details:- Date: ___/___/___ **Location: _______________________** **Bird Variant: _____________________**	**Details:- Date: ___/___/___** **Location: _______________________** **Bird Variant: _____________________**

Bird Name: Grouses	**Bird Name: Guineafowl**
Identified ☐	Identified ☐
Where seen? On the:	Where seen? On the:
Ground ☐ Plant ☐ Bush ☐ Tree ☐	Ground ☐ Plant ☐ Bush ☐ Tree ☐
Flying ☐ Dead ☐	Flying ☐ Dead ☐
Male ☐ Female ☐ Adult ☐ Chick ☐	Male ☐ Female ☐ Adult ☐ Chick ☐
Details:- Date: ___/___/___ **Location: _____________________** **Bird Variant: __________________**	**Details:- Date: ___/___/___** **Location: _____________________** **Bird Variant: __________________**
Bird Name: Gulls	**Bird Name: Hammerkop**
Identified ☐	Identified ☐
Where seen? On the:	Where seen? On the:
Ground ☐ Plant ☐ Bush ☐ Tree ☐	Ground ☐ Plant ☐ Bush ☐ Tree ☐
Flying ☐ Dead ☐	Flying ☐ Dead ☐
Male ☐ Female ☐ Adult ☐ Chick ☐	Male ☐ Female ☐ Adult ☐ Chick ☐
Details:- Date: ___/___/___ **Location: _____________________** **Bird Variant: __________________**	**Details:- Date: ___/___/___** **Location: _____________________** **Bird Variant: __________________**
Bird Name: Harriers	**Bird Name: Hawks**
Identified ☐	Identified ☐
Where seen? On the:	Where seen? On the:
Ground ☐ Plant ☐ Bush ☐ Tree ☐	Ground ☐ Plant ☐ Bush ☐ Tree ☐
Flying ☐ Dead ☐	Flying ☐ Dead ☐
Male ☐ Female ☐ Adult ☐ Chick ☐	Male ☐ Female ☐ Adult ☐ Chick ☐
Details:- Date: ___/___/___ **Location: _____________________** **Bird Variant: __________________**	**Details:- Date: ___/___/___** **Location: _____________________** **Bird Variant: __________________**

Bird Name: Heron	**Bird Name: Honeyguides**
Identified ☐	Identified ☐
Where seen? On the:	Where seen? On the:
Ground ☐ Plant ☐ Bush ☐ Tree ☐	Ground ☐ Plant ☐ Bush ☐ Tree ☐
Flying ☐ Dead ☐	Flying ☐ Dead ☐
Male ☐ Female ☐ Adult ☐ Chick ☐	Male ☐ Female ☐ Adult ☐ Chick ☐
Details:- Date: ___/___/___ **Location: ______________________** **Bird Variant: ___________________**	**Details:- Date: ___/___/___** **Location: ______________________** **Bird Variant: ___________________**
Bird Name: Hoopoes	**Bird Name: Hornbills**
Identified ☐	Identified ☐
Where seen? On the:	Where seen? On the:
Ground ☐ Plant ☐ Bush ☐ Tree ☐	Ground ☐ Plant ☐ Bush ☐ Tree ☐
Flying ☐ Dead ☐	Flying ☐ Dead ☐
Male ☐ Female ☐ Adult ☐ Chick ☐	Male ☐ Female ☐ Adult ☐ Chick ☐
Details:- Date: ___/___/___ **Location: ______________________** **Bird Variant: ___________________**	**Details:- Date: ___/___/___** **Location: ______________________** **Bird Variant: ___________________**
Bird Name: Ibises	**Bird Name: Icterids**
Identified ☐	Identified ☐
Where seen? On the:	Where seen? On the:
Ground ☐ Plant ☐ Bush ☐ Tree ☐	Ground ☐ Plant ☐ Bush ☐ Tree ☐
Flying ☐ Dead ☐	Flying ☐ Dead ☐
Male ☐ Female ☐ Adult ☐ Chick ☐	Male ☐ Female ☐ Adult ☐ Chick ☐
Details:- Date: ___/___/___ **Location: ______________________** **Bird Variant: ___________________**	**Details:- Date: ___/___/___** **Location: ______________________** **Bird Variant: ___________________**

Bird Name: Illadopses	Bird Name: Indigobirds
Identified ☐	Identified ☐
Where seen? On the:	Where seen? On the:
Ground ☐ Plant ☐ Bush ☐ Tree ☐	Ground ☐ Plant ☐ Bush ☐ Tree ☐
Flying ☐ Dead ☐	Flying ☐ Dead ☐
Male ☐ Female ☐ Adult ☐ Chick ☐	Male ☐ Female ☐ Adult ☐ Chick ☐
Details:- Date: ___/___/___ **Location:** ________________ **Bird Variant:** _______________	**Details:- Date:** ___/___/___ **Location:** ________________ **Bird Variant:** _______________
Bird Name: Jacana	**Bird Name: Kingfishers**
Identified ☐	Identified ☐
Where seen? On the:	Where seen? On the:
Ground ☐ Plant ☐ Bush ☐ Tree ☐	Ground ☐ Plant ☐ Bush ☐ Tree ☐
Flying ☐ Dead ☐	Flying ☐ Dead ☐
Male ☐ Female ☐ Adult ☐ Chick ☐	Male ☐ Female ☐ Adult ☐ Chick ☐
Details:- Date: ___/___/___ **Location:** ________________ **Bird Variant:** _______________	**Details:- Date:** ___/___/___ **Location:** ________________ **Bird Variant:** _______________
Bird Name: Kinglets	**Bird Name: Kites**
Identified ☐	Identified ☐
Where seen? On the:	Where seen? On the:
Ground ☐ Plant ☐ Bush ☐ Tree ☐	Ground ☐ Plant ☐ Bush ☐ Tree ☐
Flying ☐ Dead ☐	Flying ☐ Dead ☐
Male ☐ Female ☐ Adult ☐ Chick ☐	Male ☐ Female ☐ Adult ☐ Chick ☐
Details:- Date: ___/___/___ **Location:** ________________ **Bird Variant:** _______________	**Details:- Date:** ___/___/___ **Location:** ________________ **Bird Variant:** _______________

Bird Name: Lapwings	**Bird Name: Larks**
Identified ☐	Identified ☐
Where seen? On the:	Where seen? On the:
Ground ☐ Plant ☐ Bush ☐ Tree ☐	Ground ☐ Plant ☐ Bush ☐ Tree ☐
Flying ☐ Dead ☐	Flying ☐ Dead ☐
Male ☐ Female ☐ Adult ☐ Chick ☐	Male ☐ Female ☐ Adult ☐ Chick ☐
Details:- Date: ___/___/___ **Location: _______________________** **Bird Variant: _____________________**	**Details:- Date: ___/___/___** **Location: _______________________** **Bird Variant: _____________________**
Bird Name: Leaf Warblers	**Bird Name: Long-Tailed Tits**
Identified ☐	Identified ☐
Where seen? On the:	Where seen? On the:
Ground ☐ Plant ☐ Bush ☐ Tree ☐	Ground ☐ Plant ☐ Bush ☐ Tree ☐
Flying ☐ Dead ☐	Flying ☐ Dead ☐
Male ☐ Female ☐ Adult ☐ Chick ☐	Male ☐ Female ☐ Adult ☐ Chick ☐
Details:- Date: ___/___/___ **Location: _______________________** **Bird Variant: _____________________**	**Details:- Date: ___/___/___** **Location: _______________________** **Bird Variant: _____________________**
Bird Name: Longclaws	**Bird Name: Longspurs**
Identified ☐	Identified ☐
Where seen? On the:	Where seen? On the:
Ground ☐ Plant ☐ Bush ☐ Tree ☐	Ground ☐ Plant ☐ Bush ☐ Tree ☐
Flying ☐ Dead ☐	Flying ☐ Dead ☐
Male ☐ Female ☐ Adult ☐ Chick ☐	Male ☐ Female ☐ Adult ☐ Chick ☐
Details:- Date: ___/___/___ **Location: _______________________** **Bird Variant: _____________________**	**Details:- Date: ___/___/___** **Location: _______________________** **Bird Variant: _____________________**

Bird Name: Martins	**Bird Name: Mockingbirds**
Identified ☐	Identified ☐
Where seen? On the:	Where seen? On the:
Ground ☐ Plant ☐ Bush ☐ Tree ☐	Ground ☐ Plant ☐ Bush ☐ Tree ☐
Flying ☐ Dead ☐	Flying ☐ Dead ☐
Male ☐ Female ☐ Adult ☐ Chick ☐	Male ☐ Female ☐ Adult ☐ Chick ☐
Details:- Date: ___/___/___ **Location: _______________________** **Bird Variant: _______________________**	**Details:- Date: ___/___/___** **Location: _______________________** **Bird Variant: _______________________**
Bird Name: Mousebirds	**Bird Name: New World Warblers**
Identified ☐	Identified ☐
Where seen? On the:	Where seen? On the:
Ground ☐ Plant ☐ Bush ☐ Tree ☐	Ground ☐ Plant ☐ Bush ☐ Tree ☐
Flying ☐ Dead ☐	Flying ☐ Dead ☐
Male ☐ Female ☐ Adult ☐ Chick ☐	Male ☐ Female ☐ Adult ☐ Chick ☐
Details:- Date: ___/___/___ **Location: _______________________** **Bird Variant: _______________________**	**Details:- Date: ___/___/___** **Location: _______________________** **Bird Variant: _______________________**
Bird Name: Nightjars	**Bird Name: Nuthatches**
Identified ☐	Identified ☐
Where seen? On the:	Where seen? On the:
Ground ☐ Plant ☐ Bush ☐ Tree ☐	Ground ☐ Plant ☐ Bush ☐ Tree ☐
Flying ☐ Dead ☐	Flying ☐ Dead ☐
Male ☐ Female ☐ Adult ☐ Chick ☐	Male ☐ Female ☐ Adult ☐ Chick ☐
Details:- Date: ___/___/___ **Location: _______________________** **Bird Variant: _______________________**	**Details:- Date: ___/___/___** **Location: _______________________** **Bird Variant: _______________________**

Bird Name: Orioles	**Bird Name: Osprey**
Identified ☐	Identified ☐
Where seen? On the:	Where seen? On the:
Ground ☐ Plant ☐ Bush ☐ Tree ☐	Ground ☐ Plant ☐ Bush ☐ Tree ☐
Flying ☐ Dead ☐	Flying ☐ Dead ☐
Male ☐ Female ☐ Adult ☐ Chick ☐	Male ☐ Female ☐ Adult ☐ Chick ☐
Details:- Date: ___/___/___ **Location: ___________________** **Bird Variant: ___________________**	**Details:- Date: ___/___/___** **Location: ___________________** **Bird Variant: ___________________**
Bird Name: Owls	**Bird Name: Oystercatchers**
Identified ☐	Identified ☐
Where seen? On the:	Where seen? On the:
Ground ☐ Plant ☐ Bush ☐ Tree ☐	Ground ☐ Plant ☐ Bush ☐ Tree ☐
Flying ☐ Dead ☐	Flying ☐ Dead ☐
Male ☐ Female ☐ Adult ☐ Chick ☐	Male ☐ Female ☐ Adult ☐ Chick ☐
Details:- Date: ___/___/___ **Location: ___________________** **Bird Variant: ___________________**	**Details:- Date: ___/___/___** **Location: ___________________** **Bird Variant: ___________________**
Bird Name: Parrots	**Bird Name: Partridges**
Identified ☐	Identified ☐
Where seen? On the:	Where seen? On the:
Ground ☐ Plant ☐ Bush ☐ Tree ☐	Ground ☐ Plant ☐ Bush ☐ Tree ☐
Flying ☐ Dead ☐	Flying ☐ Dead ☐
Male ☐ Female ☐ Adult ☐ Chick ☐	Male ☐ Female ☐ Adult ☐ Chick ☐
Details:- Date: ___/___/___ **Location: ___________________** **Bird Variant: ___________________**	**Details:- Date: ___/___/___** **Location: ___________________** **Bird Variant: ___________________**

Bird Name: Pelicans	**Bird Name: Penduline Tits**
Identified □	Identified □
Where seen? On the:	Where seen? On the:
Ground □ Plant □ Bush □ Tree □	Ground □ Plant □ Bush □ Tree □
Flying □ Dead □	Flying □ Dead □
Male □ Female □ Adult □ Chick □	Male □ Female □ Adult □ Chick □
Details:- Date: ___/___/___ **Location: __________________** **Bird Variant: _________________**	**Details:- Date: ___/___/___** **Location: __________________** **Bird Variant: _________________**
Bird Name: Petrels	**Bird Name: Pheasants**
Identified □	Identified □
Where seen? On the:	Where seen? On the:
Ground □ Plant □ Bush □ Tree □	Ground □ Plant □ Bush □ Tree □
Flying □ Dead □	Flying □ Dead □
Male □ Female □ Adult □ Chick □	Male □ Female □ Adult □ Chick □
Details:- Date: ___/___/___ **Location: __________________** **Bird Variant: _________________**	**Details:- Date: ___/___/___** **Location: __________________** **Bird Variant: _________________**
Bird Name: Piapacs	**Bird Name: Pigeons**
Identified □	Identified □
Where seen? On the:	Where seen? On the:
Ground □ Plant □ Bush □ Tree □	Ground □ Plant □ Bush □ Tree □
Flying □ Dead □	Flying □ Dead □
Male □ Female □ Adult □ Chick □	Male □ Female □ Adult □ Chick □
Details:- Date: ___/___/___ **Location: __________________** **Bird Variant: _________________**	**Details:- Date: ___/___/___** **Location: __________________** **Bird Variant: _________________**

Bird Name: Pipits	**Bird Name: Plovers**
Identified ☐	Identified ☐
Where seen? On the:	Where seen? On the:
Ground ☐ Plant ☐ Bush ☐ Tree ☐	Ground ☐ Plant ☐ Bush ☐ Tree ☐
Flying ☐ Dead ☐	Flying ☐ Dead ☐
Male ☐ Female ☐ Adult ☐ Chick ☐	Male ☐ Female ☐ Adult ☐ Chick ☐
Details:- Date: ___/___/___ **Location:** _______________________ **Bird Variant:** _______________________	**Details:- Date:** ___/___/___ **Location:** _______________________ **Bird Variant:** _______________________
Bird Name: Pratincoles	**Bird Name: Quails**
Identified ☐	Identified ☐
Where seen? On the:	Where seen? On the:
Ground ☐ Plant ☐ Bush ☐ Tree ☐	Ground ☐ Plant ☐ Bush ☐ Tree ☐
Flying ☐ Dead ☐	Flying ☐ Dead ☐
Male ☐ Female ☐ Adult ☐ Chick ☐	Male ☐ Female ☐ Adult ☐ Chick ☐
Details:- Date: ___/___/___ **Location:** _______________________ **Bird Variant:** _______________________	**Details:- Date:** ___/___/___ **Location:** _______________________ **Bird Variant:** _______________________
Bird Name: Queleas	**Bird Name: Rails**
Identified ☐	Identified ☐
Where seen? On the:	Where seen? On the:
Ground ☐ Plant ☐ Bush ☐ Tree ☐	Ground ☐ Plant ☐ Bush ☐ Tree ☐
Flying ☐ Dead ☐	Flying ☐ Dead ☐
Male ☐ Female ☐ Adult ☐ Chick ☐	Male ☐ Female ☐ Adult ☐ Chick ☐
Details:- Date: ___/___/___ **Location:** _______________________ **Bird Variant:** _______________________	**Details:- Date:** ___/___/___ **Location:** _______________________ **Bird Variant:** _______________________

Bird Name: Reed Warblers	**Bird Name: Rollers**
Identified ☐	Identified ☐
Where seen? On the:	Where seen? On the:
Ground ☐ Plant ☐ Bush ☐ Tree ☐	Ground ☐ Plant ☐ Bush ☐ Tree ☐
Flying ☐ Dead ☐	Flying ☐ Dead ☐
Male ☐ Female ☐ Adult ☐ Chick ☐	Male ☐ Female ☐ Adult ☐ Chick ☐
Details:- Date: ___/___/___ **Location: _______________________** **Bird Variant: _____________________**	**Details:- Date: ___/___/___** **Location: _______________________** **Bird Variant: _____________________**
Bird Name: Sandgrouses	**Bird Name: Sandpipers**
Identified ☐	Identified ☐
Where seen? On the:	Where seen? On the:
Ground ☐ Plant ☐ Bush ☐ Tree ☐	Ground ☐ Plant ☐ Bush ☐ Tree ☐
Flying ☐ Dead ☐	Flying ☐ Dead ☐
Male ☐ Female ☐ Adult ☐ Chick ☐	Male ☐ Female ☐ Adult ☐ Chick ☐
Details:- Date: ___/___/___ **Location: _______________________** **Bird Variant: _____________________**	**Details:- Date: ___/___/___** **Location: _______________________** **Bird Variant: _____________________**
Bird Name: Shearwaters	**Bird Name: Shrikes**
Identified ☐	Identified ☐
Where seen? On the:	Where seen? On the:
Ground ☐ Plant ☐ Bush ☐ Tree ☐	Ground ☐ Plant ☐ Bush ☐ Tree ☐
Flying ☐ Dead ☐	Flying ☐ Dead ☐
Male ☐ Female ☐ Adult ☐ Chick ☐	Male ☐ Female ☐ Adult ☐ Chick ☐
Details:- Date: ___/___/___ **Location: _______________________** **Bird Variant: _____________________**	**Details:- Date: ___/___/___** **Location: _______________________** **Bird Variant: _____________________**

Bird Name: Skimmers	**Bird Name: Skuas**
Identified ☐	Identified ☐
Where seen? On the:	Where seen? On the:
Ground ☐ Plant ☐ Bush ☐ Tree ☐	Ground ☐ Plant ☐ Bush ☐ Tree ☐
Flying ☐ Dead ☐	Flying ☐ Dead ☐
Male ☐ Female ☐ Adult ☐ Chick ☐	Male ☐ Female ☐ Adult ☐ Chick ☐
Details:- Date: ___/___/___ **Location: ____________________** **Bird Variant: __________________**	**Details:- Date: ___/___/___** **Location: ____________________** **Bird Variant: __________________**
Bird Name: Snipes	**Bird Name: Sparrows**
Identified ☐	Identified ☐
Where seen? On the:	Where seen? On the:
Ground ☐ Plant ☐ Bush ☐ Tree ☐	Ground ☐ Plant ☐ Bush ☐ Tree ☐
Flying ☐ Dead ☐	Flying ☐ Dead ☐
Male ☐ Female ☐ Adult ☐ Chick ☐	Male ☐ Female ☐ Adult ☐ Chick ☐
Details:- Date: ___/___/___ **Location: ____________________** **Bird Variant: __________________**	**Details:- Date: ___/___/___** **Location: ____________________** **Bird Variant: __________________**
Bird Name: Spoonbills	**Bird Name: Starlings**
Identified ☐	Identified ☐
Where seen? On the:	Where seen? On the:
Ground ☐ Plant ☐ Bush ☐ Tree ☐	Ground ☐ Plant ☐ Bush ☐ Tree ☐
Flying ☐ Dead ☐	Flying ☐ Dead ☐
Male ☐ Female ☐ Adult ☐ Chick ☐	Male ☐ Female ☐ Adult ☐ Chick ☐
Details:- Date: ___/___/___ **Location: ____________________** **Bird Variant: __________________**	**Details:- Date: ___/___/___** **Location: ____________________** **Bird Variant: __________________**

Bird Name: Stilts	**Bird Name: Storks**
Identified ☐	Identified ☐
Where seen? On the:	Where seen? On the:
Ground ☐ Plant ☐ Bush ☐ Tree ☐	Ground ☐ Plant ☐ Bush ☐ Tree ☐
Flying ☐ Dead ☐	Flying ☐ Dead ☐
Male ☐ Female ☐ Adult ☐ Chick ☐	Male ☐ Female ☐ Adult ☐ Chick ☐
Details:- Date: ___/___/___ **Location: ____________________** **Bird Variant: _________________**	**Details:- Date: ___/___/___** **Location: ____________________** **Bird Variant: _________________**
Details:- Date: ___/___/___ **Location: ____________________** **Bird Variant: _________________**	**Details:- Date: ___/___/___** **Location: ____________________** **Bird Variant: _________________**
Identified ☐	Identified ☐
Where seen? On the:	Where seen? On the:
Ground ☐ Plant ☐ Bush ☐ Tree ☐	Ground ☐ Plant ☐ Bush ☐ Tree ☐
Flying ☐ Dead ☐	Flying ☐ Dead ☐
Male ☐ Female ☐ Adult ☐ Chick ☐	Male ☐ Female ☐ Adult ☐ Chick ☐
Details:- Date: ___/___/___ **Location: ____________________** **Bird Variant: _________________**	**Details:- Date: ___/___/___** **Location: ____________________** **Bird Variant: _________________**
Bird Name: Swans	**Bird Name: Swifts**
Identified ☐	Identified ☐
Where seen? On the:	Where seen? On the:
Ground ☐ Plant ☐ Bush ☐ Tree ☐	Ground ☐ Plant ☐ Bush ☐ Tree ☐
Flying ☐ Dead ☐	Flying ☐ Dead ☐
Male ☐ Female ☐ Adult ☐ Chick ☐	Male ☐ Female ☐ Adult ☐ Chick ☐
Details:- Date: ___/___/___ **Location: ____________________** **Bird Variant: _________________**	**Details:- Date: ___/___/___** **Location: ____________________** **Bird Variant: _________________**

Bird Name: Tropicbirds	**Bird Name: Turacos**
Identified ☐	Identified ☐
Where seen? On the:	Where seen? On the:
Ground ☐ Plant ☐ Bush ☐ Tree ☐	Ground ☐ Plant ☐ Bush ☐ Tree ☐
Flying ☐ Dead ☐	Flying ☐ Dead ☐
Male ☐ Female ☐ Adult ☐ Chick ☐	Male ☐ Female ☐ Adult ☐ Chick ☐
Details:- Date: ___/___/___ **Location: _______________________** **Bird Variant: _____________________**	**Details:- Date: ___/___/___** **Location: _______________________** **Bird Variant: _____________________**
Bird Name: Vireos	**Bird Name: Vultures**
Identified ☐	Identified ☐
Where seen? On the:	Where seen? On the:
Ground ☐ Plant ☐ Bush ☐ Tree ☐	Ground ☐ Plant ☐ Bush ☐ Tree ☐
Flying ☐ Dead ☐	Flying ☐ Dead ☐
Male ☐ Female ☐ Adult ☐ Chick ☐	Male ☐ Female ☐ Adult ☐ Chick ☐
Details:- Date: ___/___/___ **Location: _______________________** **Bird Variant: _____________________**	**Details:- Date: ___/___/___** **Location: _______________________** **Bird Variant: _____________________**
Bird Name: Waders	**Bird Name: Wagtails**
Identified ☐	Identified ☐
Where seen? On the:	Where seen? On the:
Ground ☐ Plant ☐ Bush ☐ Tree ☐	Ground ☐ Plant ☐ Bush ☐ Tree ☐
Flying ☐ Dead ☐	Flying ☐ Dead ☐
Male ☐ Female ☐ Adult ☐ Chick ☐	Male ☐ Female ☐ Adult ☐ Chick ☐
Details:- Date: ___/___/___ **Location: _______________________** **Bird Variant: _____________________**	**Details:- Date: ___/___/___** **Location: _______________________** **Bird Variant: _____________________**

Bird Name: Wallcreepers	**Bird Name: Warblers**
Identified □	Identified □
Where seen? On the:	Where seen? On the:
Ground □ Plant □ Bush □ Tree □	Ground □ Plant □ Bush □ Tree □
Flying □ Dead □	Flying □ Dead □
Male □ Female □ Adult □ Chick □	Male □ Female □ Adult □ Chick □
Details:- Date: ___/___/___ **Location: ____________________** **Bird Variant: ________________**	**Details:- Date: ___/___/___** **Location: ____________________** **Bird Variant: ________________**
Bird Name: Waxwings	**Bird Name: Weavers**
Identified □	Identified □
Where seen? On the:	Where seen? On the:
Ground □ Plant □ Bush □ Tree □	Ground □ Plant □ Bush □ Tree □
Flying □ Dead □	Flying □ Dead □
Male □ Female □ Adult □ Chick □	Male □ Female □ Adult □ Chick □
Details:- Date: ___/___/___ **Location: ____________________** **Bird Variant: ________________**	**Details:- Date: ___/___/___** **Location: ____________________** **Bird Variant: ________________**
Bird Name: Wheatears	**Bird Name: White-Eyes**
Identified □	Identified □
Where seen? On the:	Where seen? On the:
Ground □ Plant □ Bush □ Tree □	Ground □ Plant □ Bush □ Tree □
Flying □ Dead □	Flying □ Dead □
Male □ Female □ Adult □ Chick □	Male □ Female □ Adult □ Chick □
Details:- Date: ___/___/___ **Location: ____________________** **Bird Variant: ________________**	**Details:- Date: ___/___/___** **Location: ____________________** **Bird Variant: ________________**

Bird Name: Whydahs	**Bird Name: Widowbirds**
Identified ☐	Identified ☐
Where seen? On the:	Where seen? On the:
Ground ☐ Plant ☐ Bush ☐ Tree ☐	Ground ☐ Plant ☐ Bush ☐ Tree ☐
Flying ☐ Dead ☐	Flying ☐ Dead ☐
Male ☐ Female ☐ Adult ☐ Chick ☐	Male ☐ Female ☐ Adult ☐ Chick ☐
Details:- Date: ___/___/___ **Location: _____________________** **Bird Variant: _____________________**	**Details:- Date: ___/___/___** **Location: _____________________** **Bird Variant: _____________________**
Bird Name: Woodpeckers	**Bird Name: Wrens**
Identified ☐	Identified ☐
Where seen? On the:	Where seen? On the:
Ground ☐ Plant ☐ Bush ☐ Tree ☐	Ground ☐ Plant ☐ Bush ☐ Tree ☐
Flying ☐ Dead ☐	Flying ☐ Dead ☐
Male ☐ Female ☐ Adult ☐ Chick ☐	Male ☐ Female ☐ Adult ☐ Chick ☐
Details:- Date: ___/___/___ **Location: _____________________** **Bird Variant: _____________________**	**Details:- Date: ___/___/___** **Location: _____________________** **Bird Variant: _____________________**
Bird Name: Wrynecks	**Bird Name:**
Identified ☐	Identified ☐
Where seen? On the:	Where seen? On the:
Ground ☐ Plant ☐ Bush ☐ Tree ☐	Ground ☐ Plant ☐ Bush ☐ Tree ☐
Flying ☐ Dead ☐	Flying ☐ Dead ☐
Male ☐ Female ☐ Adult ☐ Chick ☐	Male ☐ Female ☐ Adult ☐ Chick ☐
Details:- Date: ___/___/___ **Location: _____________________** **Bird Variant: _____________________**	**Details:- Date: ___/___/___** **Location: _____________________** **Bird Variant: _____________________**

Bird Name:	**Bird Name:**
Identified ☐	Identified ☐
Where seen? On the:	Where seen? On the:
Ground ☐ Plant ☐ Bush ☐ Tree ☐	Ground ☐ Plant ☐ Bush ☐ Tree ☐
Flying ☐ Dead ☐	Flying ☐ Dead ☐
Male ☐ Female ☐ Adult ☐ Chick ☐	Male ☐ Female ☐ Adult ☐ Chick ☐
Details:- Date: ___/___/___ **Location: ___________________** **Bird Variant: _________________**	**Details:- Date: ___/___/___** **Location: ___________________** **Bird Variant: _________________**
Bird Name:	**Bird Name:**
Identified ☐	Identified ☐
Where seen? On the:	Where seen? On the:
Ground ☐ Plant ☐ Bush ☐ Tree ☐	Ground ☐ Plant ☐ Bush ☐ Tree ☐
Flying ☐ Dead ☐	Flying ☐ Dead ☐
Male ☐ Female ☐ Adult ☐ Chick ☐	Male ☐ Female ☐ Adult ☐ Chick ☐
Details:- Date: ___/___/___ **Location: ___________________** **Bird Variant: _________________**	**Details:- Date: ___/___/___** **Location: ___________________** **Bird Variant: _________________**
Bird Name:	**Bird Name:**
Identified ☐	Identified ☐
Where seen? On the:	Where seen? On the:
Ground ☐ Plant ☐ Bush ☐ Tree ☐	Ground ☐ Plant ☐ Bush ☐ Tree ☐
Flying ☐ Dead ☐	Flying ☐ Dead ☐
Male ☐ Female ☐ Adult ☐ Chick ☐	Male ☐ Female ☐ Adult ☐ Chick ☐
Details:- Date: ___/___/___ **Location: ___________________** **Bird Variant: _________________**	**Details:- Date: ___/___/___** **Location: ___________________** **Bird Variant: _________________**